DON'T GIVE THE ENEMY A SEAT AT YOUR TABLE

IT'S TIME TO WIN THE BATTLE OF YOUR MIND . . .

STUDY GUIDE
BASED ON PSALM 23

LOUIE GIGLIO

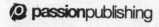

W PUBLISHING GROUP

AN IMPRINT OF THOMAS NELSON

Published in Nashville, Tennessee, by W Publishing Group, an imprint of Thomas Nelson. W Publishing Group and Thomas Nelson are registered trademarks of HarperCollins Christian Publishing, Inc.

All Scripture quotations are taken from the *New International Version®*, NIV®. Copyright © 1973, 1978, 1984, 2011 by Biblica, Inc.® Used by permission. All rights reserved worldwide.

Thomas Nelson titles may be purchased in bulk for educational, business, fundraising, or sales promotional use. For information, please e-mail SpecialMarkets@ ThomasNelson.com.

ISBN 978-0-310-13424-4 (softcover)
ISBN 978-0-310-13425-1 (ebook)

First Printing March 2021

Printed in the United States of America

CONTENTS

INTRODUCTION

Every day we fight a battle against an enemy who wants to wage war in our minds. At home and at work, at school and at church, in our neighborhoods and in our communities, we are faced with a barrage of demands, distractions, responsibilities, obligations, and perspectives. The relentless assault of so many forces competing for our attention can be overwhelming.

Perhaps the greatest casualty in this battle is our own peace. We worry, feel edgy and anxious, and give in to fears or doubts. We seek comfort in old habits to find temporary relief from the battle fatigue. We might even feel guilty for having these struggles, thinking that if only we had a *stronger faith* we wouldn't feel unsettled so often. Our self-assessment only makes us feel worse and leaves us feeling more weary, uncertain, and frustrated.

The good news is that we don't have to live in this mental war zone! We have the power, through Jesus Christ, to defeat the enemy and take authority over our minds. We can take back our freedom and control our thoughts and emotions. We can overcome feelings of fear, despair, and frustration. We have been invited into an intimate relationship with the Almighty. We don't need to wrestle any longer with harmful and negative thoughts. As Jesus said, "Come to me, all you who are weary and burdened, and I will give you rest" (Matthew 11:28).

In Psalm 23, David wrote that God will not only guide and shepherd us through life but will also protect and provide for us along the way. "You prepare a table before me in the presence of my enemies . . . Surely your goodness and love will follow me all the days of my life, and I will dwell in the house of the LORD forever" (Psalm 23:5–6). God has prepared a table for us—a table for two—set with an abundance of peace, clarity, and purpose.

It's worth noting before we go too much further on this journey together that this table is set for *two*. Our enemy, the devil, is not intended to join us there. That's why we can't *give the enemy a seat at our table!* Instead, we must allow our Good Shepherd to lead us through the dark valleys into green pastures and quiet waters where He has prepared a banquet for us. His invitation is to linger at this table and find nourishment, rest, and deep intimacy with the King of the Universe.

It's time to win the battle for your mind. *Are you ready?* Let's jump in and begin.

HOW TO USE THIS GUIDE

GROUP SIZE

This six-session video Bible study is designed to be experienced in a group setting such as a Bible study, Sunday school class, or other small-group gathering. If your gathering is large, you may want to consider splitting everyone into smaller groups of five or six people. This will ensure that everyone has enough time to participate in discussions.

MATERIALS NEEDED

Everyone in your group will need a copy of this study guide, which includes the opening questions to discuss, notes for the video teachings, directions for activities and discussion questions, and personal studies in between sessions. We also encourage you to get a copy of the book *Don't Give the Enemy a Seat at Your Table*, which will provide further insights into the material you are covering in this study. To aid your study experience, you will be asked to read specific chapters in the book to prepare for the group's next meeting.

FACILITATION

Your group will need to appoint a person to serve as a facilitator. This person will be responsible for starting the video and keeping track of time during discussions and activities. Facilitators may also read questions aloud and monitor discussions, prompting everyone in the group to respond and assuring that everyone has the opportunity to participate. If you have been chosen for this role, note that there are additional instructions and resources in the back of this guide to help you lead your group members through the study.

PERSONAL STUDIES

During the week, you can maximize the impact of this course with the personal studies provided. Treat each personal study like a devotional and use them in whatever way works best for your schedule. You could do one section each day for three days of the week or complete them all in one sitting. These personal studies are not intended to be burdensome or time-consuming but to provide a richer experience and continuity in between your group sessions.

THE TABLE BEFORE US

Read

The enemy wants to crush you. He wants to steal from you everything you value. He wants to kill everything in your life that's good. He wants to destroy you. If he can claim the victory over your mind, he can claim the victory over your life. But you don't have to let him get a foothold. For you have been invited to an intimate relationship with the Almighty. Your Good Shepherd has set a table before you . . . and the enemy has not been invited to join.

LOUIE GIGLIO
—FROM CHAPTER 1 OF *DON'T GIVE THE ENEMY A SEAT AT YOUR TABLE*

WELCOME

Have you ever sent a text in the heat of the moment? Maybe you are dealing with a situation where someone at work takes credit for your idea. Or perhaps you are facing yet *another* argument with a family member. Or maybe it is neighborhood gossip, divisions in your church, or aggressive online posts that cause you a level of angst.

Whatever the situation, it stirs up feelings of defensiveness, insecurity, frustration, or even anger within you. So you reach out to a trusted friend, family member, or confidante with a text to recount the latest strike in your battle. Your hope, of course, is that the person will come alongside you in your dismay and frustration and offer a show of support. You want to be affirmed . . . and you know you can count on your supporter to reinforce your viewpoint.

You're eager for the validation your ally can provide. You stare at your phone as you see the signal that your text is being read. You wait for the response to come through. But when it does, it is not at all what you expected. Your wise confidante simply tells you to not allow the other person to lead you into harboring feelings of hostility, resentment, and bitterness.

Your initial reaction is disappointment, followed by anger and confusion. What is your friend talking about? Didn't they read your message? Doesn't your friend understand how you are feeling? But suddenly, your perspective shifts. You recognize the gift you've just been given. Your friend's response may not have been what you expected, but it was certainly what you *needed*. The roiling emotions and jumbled thoughts weren't really about the situation that caused your rant. No, they were about what is going on in your *soul*.

You are in a spiritual battle, and the enemy is trying to wedge his seeds of doubt, fear, anger, and distrust into your consciousness. He is trying to get a seat at the "table" of your mind so he can lead you down paths he wants you to travel on. The good news is that you don't have to go there. You can win this battle. But first, you have to recognize what you're up against.

SHARE

If you or any of your group members are just getting to know one another, take a few minutes to introduce yourselves. Then, to get things started, discuss one of the following questions:

- On average, how many texts do you send or respond to each day? Is texting more of a convenience for you or an intrusion?

— o r —

- Have you found yourself in a situation like the one described in the opening story? If so, how did you react? What was the result of your actions?

READ

Have someone read aloud Psalm 23. While these words may be familiar to you, try to imagine that you are hearing them for the first time.

> [1] The LORD is my shepherd, I lack nothing.
> [2] He makes me lie down in green pastures,
>   he leads me beside quiet waters,
> [3] he refreshes my soul.
> He guides me along the right paths
>   for his name's sake.
> [4] Even though I walk
>   through the darkest valley,
> I will fear no evil,
>   for you are with me;
> your rod and your staff,
>   they comfort me.
> [5] You prepare a table before me
>   in the presence of my enemies.
> You anoint my head with oil;
>   my cup overflows.
> [6] Surely your goodness and love will follow me
>   all the days of my life,
> and I will dwell in the house of the LORD
>   forever.

What image or description stands out the most to you in this psalm? Why?

Did you grow up hearing this psalm or perhaps memorize it when you were young? What personal associations do you have with this passage? Memories

What is it about Psalm 23 that people find so comforting and reassuring? How did it make you feel when you heard it just now?

WATCH

Play the video segment for session one. As you watch, use the following outline to record any thoughts or concepts that stand out to you.

"Don't give the enemy a seat at your table." Those nine words can change your life. Don't allow the enemy access to your conversations, thoughts, attitudes, or emotions. Don't allow the enemy into your story. You will only end up having a conversation with a killer.

Psalm 23 is perhaps the most beloved and well-known psalm of all time. But this is not a soft, fluffy, spiritual lullaby. David, a warrior and the king of Israel, drew on his gritty experience shepherding sheep as a youth to express a powerful metaphor about how we relate to God. *See God deliver —*

"The LORD is my shepherd" (Psalm 23:1). You were created to be led. If God is not leading you, it means you are being led by someone else. If you think *you* are leading your life—calling the shots—then congratulations . . . you are your own shepherd!

Created to be led!

"I shall not be in want" (Psalm 23:1 NIV 84). David didn't always get what he wanted every day. But he never lacked what he needed any day of his life.

"He makes me lie down in green pastures" (Psalm 23:2). When Jesus makes you do something, it's for your own good. You—His sheep—need guidance and rest. Sometimes, He uses His shepherd's crook to get you moving in the right direction.

Need help. Makes for break + rest green pasture we need.

David's words in Psalm 23:3–5 describe your faith as you learn to trust your Good Shepherd. He will guide you in paths of righteousness. He will be with you as you walk through the valley of the shadow of death. His rod and staff will comfort you. He will anoint your head with oil. *lead restore guide*

"Surely your goodness and love will follow me all the days of my life, and I will dwell in the house of the LORD forever" (Psalm 23:6). This is the capstone of the psalm. You can count on God's goodness and love to follow you all the days of your life. This is what you get when you trade whatever shepherd that you've been following for Jesus leading your life.

"You prepare a table before me in the presence of my enemies" (Psalm 23:5). God will not extract you from a broken world. Rather, He sets a table for two in the presence of your enemies. You have been invited to dine with the King in the middle of the battlefield.

persecution - right in middle
Table with the King -
Accept this intimacy with the Almighty --

DISCUSS

Take a few minutes within your group to discuss what you just watched and explore these concepts in Scripture.

1. According to Psalm 23, what are the attributes of your Good Shepherd? What does He promise to provide? How have you seen these traits in the way that Jesus leads you?

2. How do you feel about being compared to sheep in this psalm (see also Matthew 18:12–14; Luke 15:4–7; 1 Peter 2:25)? In what ways does this comparison ring true based on your life experience? In what ways do you struggle to accept this comparison?

3. What are some of the "bad" shepherds in your life? Why is it often so tempting to follow after them? In what ways are you tempted to be your *own* shepherd?

4. David didn't always get what he *wanted* every day of his life. But he never lacked what he *needed* any day of his life. How would you define the difference between the two?

5. How does your Good Shepherd make you lie down in green pastures? What does this look like in your life? Are you allowing Him to lead you in this area?

6. What comes to mind when you imagine the Good Shepherd preparing a table for you in the presence of your enemies? What does your "battlefield" look like at the moment? Why is it important that your enemies are *present* but not *invited to sit* at your table?

RESPOND

Briefly review the outline for the session one teaching and any notes you took. In the space below, write down the most significant point you took away from this session.

PRAY

End your session by sharing any requests that you would like the group to lift up in prayer. Thank God for bringing you together for this study so you can draw closer to Him and win the battle for your mind. Ask your Good Shepherd to help you recognize his voice in your life and focus on his ways instead of your own—and definitely not the enemy's ways.

BETWEEN-SESSIONS PERSONAL STUDY

This week's group discussion is just the start, and we want you to keep digging into how you can claim the victory for your mind. So we've created this section as a guide for your personal study time to further explore the topics you discussed with your group. Before you begin, read or review chapters one and two in *Don't Give the Enemy a Seat at Your Table*. Note that there will be an opportunity at your next group session to share any responses or thoughts that you have.

CONNECT

Check in with your group members during the upcoming week and continue the discussion you had with them at your last gathering. Grab coffee or dinner, or reach out by text and share what's going on in your heart. Use the following questions to help guide your conversation.

What are some key words and phrases that have continued to stand out to you from Psalm 23? Why have those especially continued to resonate with you?

When have you experienced a situation in which you became aware of the enemy's presence at your "table"? How did you handle it?

How do you wish you had handled this situation? What would you do differently if you were able to do it over again?

REFLECT

Act

Winning the battle for your thoughts requires time, attention, and deliberation. In this first session, you started the process by exploring Psalm 23 and considering what it means to dine at God's table as you follow Jesus, your Good Shepherd. You've also started thinking about ways that you might be leaving space for the enemy to sit at your table.

This process requires you to become a better listener—to learn to recognize God's voice in your life. As Jesus said, "[The shepherd] calls his own sheep by name and leads them out. When he has brought out all his own, he goes on ahead of them, and his sheep follow because they know his voice" (John 10:3–4). So, consider how well you know your Good Shepherd's voice. How do you recognize it when you hear it? Spend a couple minutes in silence, stilling your heart before God as you ponder this question, and then answer the following questions.

What are some of the ways that you hear God's voice? Do you hear it more when you spend time in His Word, or during your prayer times, or through the words and actions of a fellow believer in Christ?

In Psalm 23, David describes God as a Good Shepherd who provides for our needs. David carries out this metaphor by noting the Lord makes him "lie down in green pastures," leads him "beside quiet waters," and refreshes his soul (Psalm 23:2–3). What are the most common obstacles you encounter to spending more time with your Good Shepherd in "green pastures" and resting "beside quiet waters"? What steps can you take to change that?

When have you experienced the kind of soul rest and spiritual refreshment that David describes in Psalm 23? What impact did these experiences have on your life?

Worship

Translating the original languages of the Bible have always presented challenges for scholars . . . but also unique benefits. Most biblical translations seek to balance the idea or message of the original text in expressing God's truth with the stylistic elements—such as diction, syntax, figures of speech, and poetic devices. One of the advantages of comparing such different renderings is often a deeper and richer perspective on God's Word.

Given that the psalms are primarily songs and poems, comparing translations can be especially helpful. Some images and descriptions may not seem to work together until you look at the psalm from different linguistic angles. Others, like Psalm 23, may be so familiar that they lose their meaning over time once committed to memory. With this in mind, today you will compare the text of this psalm from one of the oldest and most famous translations, the King James Version, alongside a more contemporary paraphrase, *The Message*.

Read through both versions slowly and thoughtfully, underlining key words and phrases you want to compare. Use the questions that follow to help you gain a better perspective on this timeless, beautiful, gritty psalm and its application to your life. Make your study of these two versions a time of worshiping God and thanking Him for all He provides for you.

PSALM 23 (KING JAMES VERSION)

¹ *The* LORD *is my shepherd; I shall not want.*

² *He maketh me to lie down in green pastures: he leadeth
me beside the still
waters.*

³ *He restoreth my soul: he leadeth me in the paths of
righteousness for his
name's sake.*

⁴ *Yea, though I walk through the valley of the shadow of
death, I will fear
no evil: for thou art with me; thy rod and thy staff
they comfort me.*

⁵ *Thou preparest a table before me in the presence of mine
enemies: thou
anointest my head with oil; my cup runneth over.*

⁶ *Surely goodness and mercy shall follow me all the days of
my life:
and I will dwell in the house of the* LORD *for ever.*

PSALM 23 (THE MESSAGE)

1–3 GOD, my shepherd!
  I don't need a thing.
You have bedded me down in lush meadows,
  you find me quiet pools to drink from.
True to your word,
  you let me catch my breath
  and send me in the right direction.

4 Even when the way goes through
  Death Valley,
I'm not afraid
  when you walk at my side.
Your trusty shepherd's crook
  makes me feel secure.

5 You serve me a six-course dinner
  right in front of my enemies.
You revive my drooping head;
  my cup brims with blessing.
6 Your beauty and love chase after me
  every day of my life.
I'm back home in the house of GOD
  for the rest of my life.

Which particular word choices, phrases, and descriptions did you underline in each of these translations? Why did you select those parts of the passage?

What stood out to you the most about the different ways these translations express the same ideas? Why did those items stand out to you?

Which version resonates with you more at this point in your life? Why?

DEEPER

Our Good Shepherd Is Always Near

"Even though I walk through the darkest valley, I will fear no evil, for you are with me" (Psalm 23:4). It's amazing that our Good Shepherd walks with us right through the valley of the shadow

of death. God is there with us through real hardship. He's with us when a loved one gets sick. He's with us when we bury someone we care for. He's close when our heart is shattered. He's close when we lose some sort of good thing we'd hoped for.

Maybe you're experiencing the death of a relationship or the loss of a dream. You tried to get into a certain program, but it didn't work out. You were heading for a certain job but didn't get it. You were positive a certain person was interested in you, but it turned out that person wanted to be only friends. Maybe you and your spouse were trying to conceive a child, but that window has closed.

We can experience any number of losses in the valley of the shadow of death. Loss is a part of our story as humans. We all walk through grief, disappointment, and discouragement. That's why it's so key that *even though* King David walked through such great difficulty, he declared, "I *will* fear no evil." The Good Shepherd was there to guide and comfort him.

How can we honestly say we're not afraid? The answer is shown in the second part the verse: "for you are with me." We won't solve all the problems around us. We don't avoid every problem that comes our way. Yet we don't need to fear any evil, because the Good Shepherd is with us. His rod and staff comfort us.

Let's not rush by this truth. Look at it slowly. Carefully. God Almighty *is with us*.

No matter the troubles you're walking through right now, the good news is not simply that God will help you. That's not the whole message. The message is that God *is with you*. He's with you in the sickness. He's with you at the grave. He's with you when the job opportunity doesn't come through. He's with you when you receive hard news. He's with you in the chemo ward. He's with you in the storm, and in the wind, and in the trial, and in the valley. God Almighty—your Good Shepherd—is right there in the midst of every difficulty with you.

—FROM *DON'T GIVE THE ENEMY A SEAT AT YOUR TABLE*

What currently represents the "darkest valley" in your life?

What is your prayer to God as you walk through this valley?

How does it help you to know that your Good Shepherd has promised to be with you?

For Next Week: Before your group's next session, read chapters 3 and 4 in *Don't Give the Enemy a Seat at Your Table.*

THE TACTICS OF THE ENEMY

The devil's goals are always the same. He wants to gain access to your mind so he can destroy you. He wants to get inside your head so he can plant harmful thoughts within you. He wants to steal everything valuable from you. He wants to kill your relationship with God. He wants to cause division between you and the people who care for you. It is up to you to keep him from sitting at your table. You have the power to exercise faith to defy the devil's whisper.

LOUIE GIGLIO
—FROM CHAPTER 3 OF *DON'T GIVE THE ENEMY A SEAT AT YOUR TABLE*

WELCOME

Imagine it is noon and you are sitting with a coworker in your company's lunchroom. This coworker has an important matter to discuss with you, and you've set aside some time so the two of you can focus on it. You are looking forward to getting the matter resolved.

Suddenly, from across the room, you hear your name being called. Your heart sinks. You recognize the voice. It's another coworker. One who likes to talk a lot and dominate conversations. You don't want to engage with this person at the moment, so you try to ignore it. Maybe the person will get the hint and walk away.

Nope. You hear the voice again, but this time a little louder and closer. You put on a forced smile as the intruder arrives at your table. The person stands there, grinning at you. You look up and say hello. You tip your head toward the other person already sitting with you. You mention the two of you have scheduled this time to discuss an important matter. You hope this will clue in the unwanted "guest" to move along and find another place in the lunchroom.

No such luck. Instead, the person starts talking about a project that he is working on, how unfair his boss is being, and what so-and-so did that made him mad. You quickly realize it's time to take a more direct approach. You reiterate that you and your coworker are discussing an important matter and politely ask to be left alone. But instead of departing, the intruder takes a seat next to you. "Really? I'd be happy to help. Tell me all about it."

Your enemy can be very much like this unwanted guest. He seeks to interrupt your time with the One who matters most. He wants to get a place at your table. He will try to weasel his way there and make you think he was invited. You have to know his tactics so you can resist him.

SHARE

Take some time to share at least one key takeaway or insight you had from this week's personal studies. Then, to get things started, discuss one of the following questions:

- How do you typically handle situations like the one described above? Do you tend to be more accommodating or resistant to such unwelcome visitors?

— o r —

- What are some ways that you have seen the enemy act like this unwanted coworker? How does he try to take a seat at your table?

READ

Ask someone in the group to read aloud the following passage from Luke 4:1–13. Look for the tactics that Satan used in this scene and how Jesus responded to the attacks.

¹ *Jesus, full of the Holy Spirit, left the Jordan and was led by the Spirit into the wilderness,* ² *where for forty days he was tempted by the devil. He ate nothing during those days, and at the end of them he was hungry.*

³ *The devil said to him, "If you are the Son of God, tell this stone to become bread."*

⁴ *Jesus answered, "It is written: 'Man shall not live on bread alone.'"*

⁵ *The devil led him up to a high place and showed him in an instant all the kingdoms of the world.* ⁶ *And he said to him, "I will give you all their authority and splendor; it has been given to me, and I can give it to anyone I want to.* ⁷ *If you worship me, it will all be yours."*

⁸ *Jesus answered, "It is written: 'Worship the Lord your God and serve him only.'"*

⁹ *The devil led him to Jerusalem and had him stand on the highest point of the temple. "If you are the Son of God," he said, "throw yourself down from here.* ¹⁰ *For it is written:*

> *"'He will command his angels concerning you*
> *to guard you carefully;*
> ¹¹ *they will lift you up in their hands,*
> *so that you will not strike your foot against a stone.'"*

¹² *Jesus answered, "It is said: 'Do not put the Lord your God to the test.'"*

¹³ *When the devil had finished all this tempting, he left him until an opportune time.*

What surprises you most in this interaction between Jesus and Satan? Why?

What tactics did Satan try to use against Jesus? Why do you think he chose this approach?

How did Jesus respond to each of Satan's temptations? What is the implication for you?

WATCH

Play the video segment for session two. As you watch, use the following outline to record any thoughts or concepts that stand out to you.

God is inviting us to enter into a relationship with Him and dine with Him at His table. But it's amazing how quickly the enemy will try to take a seat there! He is persistent, persuasive, and only needs a tiny opportunity to pull up a seat and interrupt your time with the King.

1 Peter 5:8   tiny opportunity

fear, frustration

The enemy is always prowling around, looking for a way to have a place at the table—and we let him sit there. Before we know it, we are agreeing with all of the lies that he is speaking to us. The slightest crack of doubt, fear, frustration, or angst can give him access to our lives.

There are four ways to know the enemy is at our table. The first is if we are entertaining the idea that **it's better at another table**. Jesus said the thief comes only to steal, kill, and destroy. Satan will plant lies to make us believe that we are not experiencing the abundant life that Jesus has to offer—things would be better if we were in a different situation.

John 10:10

A second way to know the enemy is at our table is if we find ourselves thinking that **we are not going to make it**. Our Good Shepherd has promised to be with us and see us through even the valley of the shadow of death. His army is actually surrounding us.

I will fear no evil

As our narrative lead them through

A third way to know the enemy is at our table is if we are hearing that **we are not good enough**. Jesus says the Good Shepherd lays down His life for the sheep. Our invitation to God's table cost Jesus everything. We have incredible value in God's eyes.

A fourth way to know the enemy is at our table is if we are believing that **everyone is against us**. Satan tells us we must go through life "closed-fist." But Jesus opened His hands for us on the cross. He gave up His life for our sakes so that we will know He is for us, not against us.

Paranoia —

Taking authority

We can move through life out of the spirit of abundance from our Good Shepherd rather than a spirit of scarcity from our enemy. As we do this, we allow the abundance of God to flow out of our lives and impact the people around us.

We cannot stop the enemy from prowling around and seeking to destroy us. But we can refuse to allow him a seat at our table. We do this by locking our eyes on our King and locking on to what He says is true about us. We take Him at His word and believe what He says about us.

Take authority over our life

DISCUSS

Take a few minutes within your group to discuss what you just watched and explore these concepts in Scripture.

1. What are some ways you have experienced the enemy inviting himself to sit at your table? What are some of the lies he has tried to plant in your thinking to undermine your faith, joy, and peace?

2. How often do you compare yourself or aspects of your life to that of other people? Are there things you tend to compare more than others? What is the cumulative impact of thinking the "grass is always greener on the other side"?

3. When have you felt powerless in trying to make certain changes in your life? How has the enemy used your attempts and failures to get in your head and make you feel you will never change? How does such negativity affect your identity and self-worth?

4. What are some areas in your life where you feel that you are not good enough or don't measure up to expectations? How do these represent lies from the enemy?

5. Can you think of a time in your life when it seemed like people were against you? Did this prove to be the reality of the situation? What did you learn as a result?

6. Which of the enemy's tactics tends to trip you the most? Knowing that you know this may be a particular area of vulnerability for you, how can you better prepare and defend yourself against the devil's relentless assault?

RESPOND

Briefly review the outline for the session two teaching and any notes you took. In the space below, write down your most significant takeaway from this session.

PRAY

End your session by sharing any requests that you would like the group to lift up in prayer. Thank God for His presence in your life, and ask Him to remind you often of His truth so you may see and clearly identify any ways that you've allowed the devil to sit at your table. Pray for power to combat the devil's deceptions as you focus on drawing closer to the love of Christ.

BETWEEN-SESSIONS PERSONAL STUDY

Continue exploring the concepts you discussed during this week's group meeting by engaging in the following exercises for your personal study time. Be sure to write down any key points that stand out to you so you can share at the next meeting.

CONNECT

Check in with your group members during the upcoming week and continue the discussion you had with them at your last gathering. Grab coffee or dinner, or reach out by text and share what's going on in your heart. Use the following questions to help guide your conversation about how to actively resist giving the enemy a seat at your table.

Think back on what you have read in *Don't Give the Enemy a Seat at Your Table* and learned in the two group sessions that you've attended so far. At this point in your journey, what key truths and biblical concepts have especially stood out to you as you seek to remove the enemy's presence at your table?

What is the greatest challenge in your life when it comes to refusing to give the enemy a seat at your table? Why is that?

How has the group experience enriched this study? Does it help knowing that others are wrestling with similar issues and snares from the enemy as you are? Why or why not?

REFLECT

Act

You need to be aware of the tactics the enemy uses against you in order to successfully turn him away from your table. One of the best ways to do this is to contrast the lies he tries to plant in your mind with the contrasting truth of God's Word. Read through the following statements that represent common lies the enemy will try to convince you are true, and then circle the ones that seem to be currently at work in your mind. Next, look up the corresponding passage for each lie you circled, and then answer the questions that follow.

Lie from the enemy	Truth from God's Word
I am weak and powerless.	God's strength is more than sufficient (2 Corinthians 12:9).
I am unlovable to God and others.	God loves you with an everlasting love (Jeremiah 31:3).
I can't be used by God because of my past.	God has blotted out the sins of your past (Romans 8:1–2).
I am worthless and irrelevant.	You are God's treasure (Deuteronomy 7:6).
I am rejected and abandoned.	God has adopted you into His own family (Ephesians 1:5).
I am deficient and incomplete.	God has made you whole and complete (Colossians 2:10).
I am alone and no one cares about me.	God cares about you and is with you (1 Peter 5:7).
I can't have peace in my life.	God will give you His perfect peace (John 14:27).
I have no purpose in this life.	God has great plans for you (Jeremiah 29:11).
I am ordinary and average.	You are extraordinary and unique (Psalm 139:14).

Based on the statements you circled, which thoughts and feelings do you struggle with the most? How does the enemy use them against you?

Which truth or passage of Scripture resonates most with where you are right now? What would change if you believed this truth and acted on it rather than the devil's lies?

This is by no means a comprehensive list. What other lies from the enemy have you bought into? What passage of Scripture could you use to combat that lie?

Worship

The enemy is an expert at playing off our vulnerabilities. It is not a coincidence that he launched his barrage of temptations at Jesus when He was alone and hungry in the desert. Today, he does the same thing—attacking us at our weakest point. If he can convince us that we are outnumbered, isolated, and powerless, he can create the tiniest "crack" he needs to infiltrate our lives. As we have seen, one of the best ways to counter these attacks is to know the truth of what God *actually* says about us based on His Word. With this in mind, read through the following passage from Romans 8:31–35, 37–39, and then answer the questions that follow.

> [31] *What, then, shall we say in response to these things? If God is for us, who can be against us?* [32] *He who did not spare his own Son, but gave him up for us all—how will he not also, along with him, graciously give us all things?* [33] *Who will bring any charge against those whom God has chosen? It is God who justifies.* [34] *Who then is the one who condemns? No one. Christ Jesus who died—more than that, who was raised to life—is at the right hand of God and is also interceding for us.* [35] *Who shall separate us from the love of Christ? Shall trouble or hardship or persecution or famine or nakedness or danger or sword?*
>
> [37] *No, in all these things we are more than conquerors through him who loved us.* [38] *For I am convinced that neither death nor life, neither angels nor demons, neither the present nor the future, nor any powers,* [39] *neither height nor depth, nor anything else in all creation, will be able to separate us from the love of God that is in Christ Jesus our Lord.*

How does Paul view the battle that you face against the enemy of your soul? What does it mean for you that God has the upper hand in whatever confrontation comes your way?

What was God willing to give up to have a relationship with you? What does this say about the lengths that He will go to protect you?

What ability does the enemy have to separate you from God's love? What does this say about the victory that you have secured in Christ?

DEEPER

Our Good Shepherd Is a Mighty Warrior

"Your rod and your staff, they comfort me" (Psalm 23:4). I grew up in a big church in downtown Atlanta. When I was twelve, I remember being in our seventh grade boys' Sunday school room. Tan linoleum floor. Cinderblock walls. Metal folding

chairs. Maps of Paul's missionary journeys on the wall. And on the far wall a big painting of the "meek and mild" Jesus.

You know the one I'm talking about. His face is pale. His robe is perfect. His hair is flawless. He has a wooly lamb on His shoulders and a crook in His hand. He is gazing off into Foreverland with a faraway look in His eyes. But Olan Mills Portrait Studios Jesus is nothing like the real thing. He's your hero. Your defender. He is the mighty Son of God!

When you are up against life and death, you need to know there's an all-powerful Good Shepherd with a rod in one hand and staff in the other. That's the Jesus of Psalm 23. That's why you find comfort in His presence. With that staff, the Good Shepherd grabs you and pulls you to safety. With that rod, He crushes any prowling lion or raging bear that charges toward you.

David, who wrote Psalm 23, had taken on a lion and a bear and pounded them into the ground. David understood what God said when He promised to be with him through the valley of the shadow of death. Jesus is there in the midst of the pressure, and He's not just standing around with His hands in His pockets. He's there to rescue us when necessary, to protect us at all costs, and to fill our cups to over-flowing. We don't need to watch over our shoulders anymore. God prepares a table for us in the midst of our enemies. Jesus is watching them, guarding us, so we can keep our attention fully fixed on the face of the Good Shepherd.

Yes, we need to know the enemy's tactics so we can spot his lies. But this is not so we can focus on the lies but so we can avoid them and fix our gaze back toward the Good Shepherd.

When we are able to spot the enemies' lies that are coming our direction, we can overcome them and win the battle for our minds with truth in Jesus' name.

—FROM CHAPTER 4 OF *DON'T GIVE THE ENEMY A SEAT AT YOUR TABLE*

What image comes into your mind when you picture Jesus as a Good Shepherd?

How has your Good Shepherd pulled you to safety in the past and protected you?

What do you do throughout your day to stay focused on your Good Shepherd?

For Next Week: Before your group's next session, read chapters 5 and 6 in *Don't Give the Enemy a Seat at Your Table.*

THE BATTLE FOR OUR MIND

You were created in the image of God. You were called to greatness. You are God's child, and He wants to set you free from anything that's holding you back. God wants you to live in the fullest potential that He has for your life. It's time you got serious about victory now that God has given you the opportunity to ask, "How is the opposition coming against me? What is the enemy doing to me? What adjustments can be made?" You can win the battle for your mind.

LOUIE GIGLIO

—FROM CHAPTER 5 OF *DON'T GIVE THE ENEMY A SEAT AT YOUR TABLE*

WELCOME

Success in life requires us to make course corrections. Entrepreneurs, thought leaders, and innovators all attest to this fact. They don't allow themselves to become discouraged by past failures. Instead, they view their mistakes as opportunities to correct their course so they can reach their goals. They view failure as inherent in the process of advancement.

Consider how this plays out on the football field. If one team is getting beaten in the first half, the coaching staff doesn't just throw in the towel at halftime. Instead, they look at the strategies their opponent successfully employed against them and come up with ways for their team to counter those tactics. They look at how their team *is* performing and focus on how they *want* the team to perform. Simply put, they change the game plan.

Successful coaches will not hesitate in making drastic and decisive shifts to their game plan if it is not working. They don't care how much effort or prep work went into developing their original plan. They don't rely on their past success and just assume that eventually things will work out if they just stay the course. Rather, they are adaptable. Such flexibility instills confidence in their players that there is a path forward to victory.

The same is true in your life and mine. Even if the enemy has taken a seat at our table, we need to recognize the "game" is not over. It is time to make the course corrections necessary for us to secure the victory that Jesus has already won on our behalf. It is time for us to realize that we are in a battle—and the fight is taking place in our mind. Once we understand this truth, we can start to change our "game plan" to counter the strategies the enemy is using against us.

SHARE

Take some time to share at least one key takeaway or insight you had from this week's personal studies. Then, to get things started, discuss one of the following questions:

- What is an activity or pursuit in your life that has required you to make course corrections? How did you put these changes in place?

— o r —

- How easy or hard is it for you to change your plans? Is this relatively easy for you to do, or do you have trouble adapting once your plans are in place?

READ

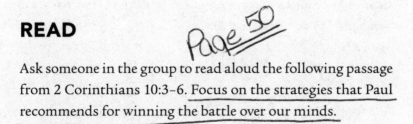

Ask someone in the group to read aloud the following passage from 2 Corinthians 10:3–6. Focus on the strategies that Paul recommends for winning the battle over our minds.

³ For though we live in the world, we do not wage war as the world does. ⁴ The weapons we fight with are not the weapons of the world. On the contrary, they have <u>divine power</u> to demolish strongholds. ⁵ <u>We demolish arguments</u> and every pretension that sets itself up against the knowledge of God, and we take captive every thought to make it obedient to Christ. ⁶ And we will be ready to punish every act of disobedience, once your obedience is complete.

What does it mean to "live in the world" but to not "wage war as the world does"?

What are some of the weapons that Paul says are available to us to use in the fight?

What comes to mind when you consider taking every thought captive in order to make it obedient to Christ? How have you attempted to do this in your life?

Prov 23:7

What we think in our hearts becomes who we are.

WATCH

Play the video segment for session three. As you watch, use the following outline to record any thoughts or key points that stand out to you. *Power to change our mind.*

What happens in the battlefield of our minds translates into our actions, decisions, and behaviors, which writes the story of who we are. We might not have the power to change our circumstances or have control over our situation. But we have the power to change our minds.

Thoughts *How we respond.*
actions
path

The coaching staff of a football team will survey what happened during the first half. When they go into the locker room at halftime, they will go over what their opponent is doing and how their team needs to react. They reiterate that they just played two quarters. But if they want to win the game, they have to make adjustments that will lead to victory in the second half.

Think right

Act right

The battle against the enemy is not about *might* but about what is *right*. It's not about wrestling him away from the table. It is about thinking *right*—what God says is true about us—and then believing that in our hearts. This is where we win the battle of the mind.

Examine every thought.

There are four key strategies to winning the battle for our mind. **First, when a thought enters our minds, we have to identify that thought and restrict access if necessary**. It has to be like a toll road, where every thought gets stopped, and we decide whether it can enter or not.

#1

Identify — — Is it of God?

We must restrict access to thoughts that are not from God. In the Garden of Eden, the enemy was able to convince Adam and Eve to sin by undermining God's heart, challenging His word, and feeding into their fears of missing out.

Set up on edge of our lives.
Undermined Gods heart
Fear of missing out.

We must make sure the thought is congruent with God's Word. This means being immersed in God's Word, living in the power of His Spirit, and surrounded by people who are the same. We kick out all thoughts that don't line up with God's Word.

Challenged Word of God
Challenged Heart of God
Fear You're going to mess out
Shortcuts
Doubts

I bind that thought in Jesus name.

#2 Second, when a thought enters our minds, **we must speak to that thought in Jesus' name**. We exercise our right as a son or a daughter of God to bind any thought that is from the enemy in Jesus' name. We either bind the thought . . . or the thought ends up binding us.

Identify and In the name of Jesus Talk back - using Gods Word -

3rd Third, when a thought enters our minds, **we must claim the truth**. Jesus taught us that we must know the Word of God so that we can combat the enemy's attempts to twist the truth. We have to know the truth so that we come against the enemy with the truth.

Know. So we can discern - know what is of God.

Reorganized =

Actions Walking Living It God

4th Fourth, when a thought enters our minds, **we must walk in the truth**. *truth*. It's not just about *knowing* God's Word but actually *living* out God's Word. This is a simple principle—God does not complicate our freedom—but it is not always easy to put into practice.

People who are like minded not from God DN line up w/ Gods Word.

Matt 4:4 Man doesn't live by bread alone
John 4:34 But by every word comes from
*   mouth of God.*

Gods word > opinion

Winning the battle for our minds means there will be fighting involved. It's a fight to identify the thought, bind it in the name of Jesus, learn the Word of God, and walk in that truth. But the promise is that we *can* win this battle for our minds . . . no matter what our past has been.

Bible concordances –

DISCUSS

Take a few minutes within your group to discuss what you just watched and explore these concepts in Scripture.

1. Why is it so critical to win the battle over your thoughts? How do you respond to the idea that regardless of what has happened in your past, you have the ability to make "halftime adjustments" that will help you secure the victory?

Did you know you have something you can do?

2. When a thought enters your mind, you first have to identify that thought to see if it is coming from the enemy or from God. How successful have you been when it comes to identifying those thoughts that are from the enemy?

Examine the thought

3. What strategies did Satan use against Adam and Eve to convince them to sin? How does he use those same tactics today to exploit any "cracks" that he can find?

She needed to examine the thought.

4. When you identify a thought that is from the enemy, how do you bind it in Jesus' name? What does this look like in actual practice in your life?

I talk to myself to God.—

5. What strategies did Jesus employ to fight against the enemy in the wilderness? What does this reveal about the importance of knowing God's Word?

6. What strategies have you found to be effective when it comes to living out the truth of God's Word? How has this helped you to win the battle for your mind?

Fighting——

RESPOND

Briefly review the outline for the session three teaching and any notes you took. In the space below, write down your most significant takeaway from this session.

PRAY

As this session comes to a close, take a moment to express any personal prayer requests that you would like to share with the group. As you pray for one another, ask God to protect you and empower you against the schemes and snares of the enemy. Thank Him for the ways that you are learning to identify and eliminate the devil's presence at your table as you complete this study. Praise Him for the gift of His Son, Jesus, and the spiritual freedom you have to defeat the enemy and enjoy intimacy with the Good Shepherd for all of eternity.

BETWEEN-SESSIONS PERSONAL STUDY

Continue exploring the concepts you discussed during this week's group meeting by engaging in the following exercises for your personal study time. Be sure to write down any key points that stand out to you so you can share at the next meeting.

CONNECT

Check in with your group members during the upcoming week and continue the discussion you had with them at your last gathering. Grab coffee or dinner, or reach out by text and share what's going on in your heart. Use the following questions to help guide your conversation about how to actively resist giving the enemy a seat at your table.

How do you usually hear from God? How often do you take time to be still before Him and focus on just listening to His voice?

What key point stood out to you from your group's last meeting? Why do you suppose that point is so significant to you at this particular time?

What are some ways you can overcome a busy schedule, interruptions, and distractions in order to spend time alone with God?

REFLECT

Act

Hearing God's voice will require you to stop *doing* and simply be *present* before God. This sounds easy, but as you know all too well, the reality is that you will encounter any number of distractions during your day that will get in the way of you spending this important time with God. So, today, the goal is to be intentional about spending this time at God's table.

Begin by silencing your phone, watch, or any other device that makes noise and could distract you. Next, set a timer on your phone for five to ten minutes. Sit in a comfortable chair in a quiet place where others won't interrupt you. Invite God to come into this space and lead you during this time. Then simply sit in silence and listen for His direction.

It is likely that a number of thoughts will barrel through your brain, some related to what you are doing ("I need to focus now on doing this") and others that seem random ("I think we're out of paper towels"). Just let them pass by and not become the center of your attention.

When your time is up, take a few moments to reflect on the experience. Use the following questions and prompts to help guide you.

What was it like to sit in silence for five minutes? What distractions came into your mind?

Did you sense that God was trying to impress anything on your heart as you spent this time alone with God?

James writes, "If any of you lacks wisdom, you should ask God, who gives generously to all" (1:5). What wisdom do you need to receive from God today?

Worship

In addition to Psalm 23, there are many other great psalms in the Bible that speak to God's character and how He promises to hear us, comfort us, protect us, and keep us from stumbling. Psalm 116, written by an unknown author, is a good case in point. As you read through verses 1–9 of this psalm, underline any words, phrases, or images that reveal the truth about God and how He promises to be with you to give you the victory. Once you have done this, read through the psalm once again, this time aloud, and then answer the questions that follow.

> ¹ I love the LORD, for he heard my voice;
>> he heard my cry for mercy.
> ² Because he turned his ear to me,
>> I will call on him as long as I live.
>
> ³ The cords of death entangled me,
>> the anguish of the grave came over me;
>> I was overcome by distress and sorrow.
> ⁴ Then I called on the name of the LORD:
>> "LORD, save me!"
>
> ⁵ The LORD is gracious and righteous;
>> our God is full of compassion.
> ⁶ The LORD protects the unwary;
>> when I was brought low, he saved me.
>
> ⁷ Return to your rest, my soul,
>> for the LORD has been good to you.

> [8] *For you, LORD, have delivered me from death,*
> *my eyes from tears,*
> *my feet from stumbling,*
> [9] *that I may walk before the LORD*
> *in the land of the living.*

Which words or phrases resonate for you the most right now? How do they address your present experience or current circumstances?

What parts of this psalm are similar to Psalm 23? How does the psalmist's words in this passage support what David wrote in Psalm 23?

What do you think the psalmist was experiencing when he wrote this poem? What contrast do you see between the challenges that he encountered and his belief in God's faithfulness?

DEEPER

Our Good Shepherd Guides Us in Life

"He guides me along the right paths for his name's sake" (Psalm 23:3). Our Good Shepherd often had to face assaults from the enemy. In the Gospels, we read how Jesus was tempted for forty days in the wilderness before His ministry even began. Day after day, the enemy sent harmful thoughts His way. Satan actually spoke to Jesus, and Jesus heard His words. Yet the Good Shepherd never chose to entertain those thoughts from the enemy.

Jesus' example reveals that when a harmful thought or temptation comes into our minds, we have a choice. We can either discard that thought or entertain it. If we discard it, good. But if we entertain it, that is when the enemy gains access to sit at our table. The sin happens when we keep hold of that harmful thought and let it take root in our minds.

Jesus taught this in the Sermon on the Mount. All sorts of folks were *entertaining* unhealthy thoughts, though they weren't always *acting* on those thoughts. They figured all was well. Jesus came along and blew this up. *Hey,* He told them, *You think you're doing fine because you're not actually murdering people. But if you hate somebody enough to want them dead . . . that's as bad as murder. You might think you're fine because you're not actually committing adultery. But guess what? If you're merely imagining yourself in an illicit relationship with someone, that's also wrong. You're committing sin with that person in your heart.*

Entertaining a harmful thought is as bad as doing a harmful deed. This is key, because it's far too easy to think we're not sinning merely because we're not acting on a sinful thought. Here's the fact: *the thought itself falls short of the glory of God.* When we entertain it, the thought muddies our relationship with the Lord. The thought itself occupies our mind and has the power to knock us off course. The frightening reality is this: once we let a harmful thought pitch a tent in our mind, eventually that temptation is acted on.

Period.

Sometimes people insist that harmful thoughts don't always lead to harmful actions. But I disagree. Harmful actions *always* begin with harmful thoughts—and harmful thoughts, harbored over time, always lead to harmful actions. Those thoughts must be stopped. If those thoughts are entertained long enough, they *will* win the battle for your mind.

—FROM CHAPTER 5 OF *DON'T GIVE THE ENEMY A SEAT AT YOUR TABLE*

Jesus was "tempted in every way, just as we are—yet he did not sin" (Hebrews 4:15). At what point does temptation lead to sin? What must take place?

Jesus was clear that entertaining a harmful thought was as bad as doing a harmful deed. What does entertaining such harmful thoughts do to our relationship with the Good Shepherd?

How do you need your Good Shepherd to guide you today when it comes to overcoming the harmful thoughts the enemy wants to plant in your mind?

For Next Week: Before your group's next session, read chapter 7 in *Don't Give the Enemy a Seat at Your Table.*

THE PATH TO VICTORY

Winning the battle for your mind requires you to take every thought captive and make it obedient to Christ. When a thought is obedient to Christ, it either aligns with Him or is rejected by Him and by God's teaching found in Scripture. If a thought is not taken captive by you in Jesus' name, that thought will take you captive. You will bind the thought, or the thought will, in time, bind you. So use the name of Jesus with authority. Bind the thoughts that don't come from God and that don't match the Word of God.

LOUIE GIGLIO
—FROM CHAPTER 7 OF *DON'T GIVE THE ENEMY A SEAT AT YOUR TABLE*

WELCOME

50%

Research shows that nearly fifty percent of the people in the United States make annual New Year's resolutions. The bulk of these relate to health and fitness, but other common resolutions include getting organized, becoming more disciplined with finances, or picking up a new skill. Yet research also reveals that fewer than *ten percent* of these people actually achieve those resolutions. They start out well, but they fail to follow through on their goals past the first few months.

less than 10% reach

So many of us can relate. We try to make positive changes in our lives, but it seems we too often end up failing—and then we feel worse about ourselves than we did before we began. It could even be the enemy has convinced us that we *cannot* and *will not* ever move from where we are to where we want to be. Maybe we realize, for the first time, that we have allowed the enemy to get a seat at our table. He has been infiltrating our thoughts and convincing us with his subtle lies that things will never be any different.

The good news is that the outcome God has planned for us is *victory* and not *defeat*. He sent His Son, Jesus, into the world to mark out the path for our success through His death on the cross and resurrection from the grave. Our Good Shepherd took on the curse of our sin, fought our fights, and overcame the enemy. While we still have battles to face, we can know that we are all overcomers and victors because of what Christ did on our behalf.

When we adapt this mindset, we begin to operate from a position of strength rather than weakness. We begin to recognize, in spite of what the enemy is telling us, that change is always possible because our Lord is always at work. As this sinks into our minds, we begin to retake ground the enemy has claimed—much like soldiers reclaiming an enemy beachhead—and push him back. We retrain our thoughts and begin to live out our story of victory.

This will not be an easy process. Reclaiming enemy territory is difficult and involves active resistance. It requires putting on the spiritual armor that God provides and waging war each day to win the battle for our minds. But in the end, we can know it is a war worth waging, for we have the promise that our ultimate victory has been secured through Christ.

SHARE

Take some time to share at least one key takeaway or insight you had from this week's personal studies. Then, to get things started, discuss one of the following questions:

- Do you typically make New Year's resolutions or set annual goals for yourself? What have you learned about yourself from such attempts?

— o r —

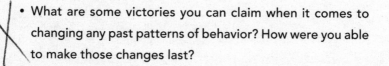

- What are some victories you can claim when it comes to changing any past patterns of behavior? How were you able to make those changes last?

READ

Ask someone in the group to read aloud the following passage from Ephesians 6:10–18. Underline or circle each piece of spiritual armor that Paul lists in these verses.

> *[10] Finally, be strong in the Lord and in his mighty power. [11] Put on the full armor of God, so that you can take your stand against the devil's schemes. [12] For our struggle is not against flesh and blood, but against the rulers, against the authorities, against the powers of this dark world and against the spiritual forces of evil in the heavenly realms. [13] Therefore put on the full armor of God, so that when the day of evil comes, you may be able to stand your ground, and after you have done everything, to stand. [14] Stand firm then, with the belt of truth buckled around your waist, with the breastplate of righteousness in place, [15] and with your feet fitted with the readiness that comes from the gospel of peace. [16] In addition to all this, take up the shield of faith, with which you can extinguish all the flaming arrows of the evil one. [17] Take the helmet of salvation and the sword of the Spirit, which is the word of God.*
>
> *[18] And pray in the Spirit on all occasions with all kinds of prayers and requests. With this in mind, be alert and always keep on praying for all the Lord's people.*

How does Paul describe the battle that is taking place for your heart and mind?

What does it mean to "put on" the armor of God?

Devils schemes

Which piece of armor do you need most in your life right now? Why?

WATCH

Play the video segment for session four. As you watch, use the following outline to record any thoughts or key points that stand out to you. *"Victory"*

God's Word tells us that our thoughts dictate the kind of people we become (see Proverbs 23:7). We can't harbor thoughts that are against God's will and expect to live a righteous life. Giving shelter and sustenance to such thoughts will lead to a different outcome.

For as a man thinks in his heart so is he.

The outcome God has planned for us is victory—to win the battle for our hearts and minds. But the enemy has a different narrative. He is going to tell us we are not going to make it, we will never succeed, and we will never measure up to whatever it is that God has put into our hearts.

Right thinking leads to right living

God has given us the victory through our Lord Jesus Christ. He has moved us from death to life spiritually. The very life of Christ has now become our life. So whatever we are facing today, it is not just us against the world. If we are in Christ, we are starting at a point of victory.

The paradox of the Christian life is that we have the victory, yet we still fight the battle. Jesus said, "It is finished" (John 19:30), but He still instructs us to fight the good fight. We must remember that we are not fighting *for* victory but are fighting *from* a place of victory.

Thief comes to steal destroy kill

Like the twelve spies who investigated the Promised Land, we often decide our own fate based on what we perceive to be our ability to win the fight in front of us. But God is telling us that He is giving us the victory. We still fight the battle, but we do so in the knowledge that God has already won.

Winning the battle of our mind begins with uniting with Jesus. We join with Him in His death in order to then join with Him in His resurrection (see Romans 6:5). We identify with Him and His suffering—and we identify with Him and His life. We are united with Christ. It's a story of victory.

It often helps if we have a daily rhythm—a method to retrain our minds that we are not in a story of defeat. Here are seven daily statements that we can make to turn our minds around during the week:

Do you have anything you need to change your mind on?

Monday: *My God knows my name* (Isaiah 43:1)

My God knows my name

Tuesday: *My God goes before me* (Deuteronomy 31:8)

fear in the hearts of people uniting with Jesus —

71

Wednesday: *I can do all things through Christ who strengthens me* (Philippians 4:13)

Thursday: *My present sufferings pale in comparison to the future glory that God has stored up for me in my life* (Romans 8:18)

Friday: *No weapon formed against me will prosper* (Isaiah 54:17)

Saturday: *I am a child of God* (Romans 8:16)

Sunday: *The same power that raised Jesus Christ from the dead lives in me* (Ephesians 1:19–20)

Allow the way that God sees you to inform how you see yourself. For how you see yourself will inform how you live and win the battle for your mind. This is the path to victory.

DISCUSS

Take a few minutes within your group to discuss what you just watched and explore these concepts in Scripture.

1. "For as [a man] thinks in his heart, so is he" (Proverbs 23:7 NKJV). What is the connection between your thoughts and your actions? How have you seen the truth of this verse play out in your life or the life of someone close to you?

2. Share a time in your life that you realized you had to make drastic changes to pursue the plans that God had for you. What factors caused you to come to this realization?

3. "But thanks be to God, who gives us the victory through our Lord Jesus Christ" (1 Corinthians 15:57). What does it mean to fight the enemy from a place of victory? How does this change your mindset regarding the spiritual battles you face?

4. God had promised to give the land of Canaan to the Israelites. However, when Moses sent twelve men to explore the land, ten came back with this report: "We seemed like grasshoppers in our own eyes, and we looked the same to them" (Numbers 13:33). What conclusions were they making about their situation that was not correct? *Impossible too BIG!*

5. Think about how your life has changed since you accepted Jesus as your Good Shepherd. What are some ways that you are now "joined" with Christ in His death and resurrection?

6. What are some of the daily rhythms you have developed to remind yourself that your story is one of victory? What Bible verse or passage of Scripture do you rely on the most often to remind yourself of God's truth in the face of the devil's deceptions? *He is the lifter of my head. Psalm 3:1-8 You o Lord are a shield*

RESPOND

Briefly review the outline for the session four teaching and any notes you took. In the space below, write down your most significant takeaway from this session.

PRAY

End your session by sharing any requests that you would like the group to lift up in prayer. Thank God for providing you with the spiritual resources that you need to defeat the enemy's assaults. Praise Him for being your Good Shepherd and for protecting you. Ask Him to continually make you aware that you are operating from a place of *victory* rather than *defeat*. Pray that He will guide you on how to counter any lies the enemy tries to plant in your mind.

Kathy
Davies family
Ukraine

BETWEEN-SESSIONS PERSONAL STUDY

Continue exploring the concepts you discussed during this week's group meeting by engaging in the following exercises for your personal study time. Be sure to write down any key points that stand out to you so you can share at the next meeting.

CONNECT

Check in with your group members during the upcoming week and continue the discussion you had with them at your last gathering. Grab coffee or dinner, or reach out by text and share what's going on in your heart. Use the following questions to help guide your conversation about how to actively resist giving the enemy a seat at your table.

How would you describe your personal path to victory over the enemy based on what you have learned so far with your group?

What are some ways you can speak God's truth into other people's lives who may be struggling with giving the enemy a seat at their table?

How are you making sure the enemy knows that he is unwelcome at your table?

REFLECT

Act

Historically, at the conclusion of a battle, the winner would often deliver a victory speech to reflect on the conflict and how the adversary was ultimately defeated. As followers of Jesus, though the battle still rages, we have already been assured of victory. So, we can likewise deliver a speech to reflect on the conflict and how we are defeating the enemy. Today, spend a few minutes writing out your victory speech to remind yourself of God's truth and how He has been with you in the midst of your darkest valley. You can fill in the blanks below to get you started or come up with your own. After you have written your draft, feel free to share it with the group at the next session.

My Victory Speech

The battle was fierce, and the enemy often tried to take me down by claiming this about me:

I could never be forgiven.

For a while, I felt like I was losing the battle because:

I believed it - hopeless

But then I remembered this truth about who God says I am:

Really repent I am forgiven made whiter than snow new creation.

I focused on this truth and put on the armor of God each day by: *Seeking Him as much as possible*

Now, the enemy has been defeated, and I live in the freedom that Jesus secured for me. Among the many blessings I experience now that the battle is won, I particularly enjoy:

In conclusion, I would like to say, "Now to him who is able to do immeasurably more than all we ask or imagine, according to his power that is at work within us, to him be glory in the church and in Christ Jesus throughout all generations, for ever and ever! Amen" (Ephesians 3:20–21).

Worship

As you've seen, one of the best ways to counter the enemy's attacks is by focusing on God's truth and the spiritual realities of who you are in Christ. God's Word reinforces this practice by reminding you to keep your mind focused on what is *holy* and *eternal* rather than on what is *worldly* and *temporary*. Keep this contrast in mind as you read the following passage from Philippians 4:4–9, and then complete the questions that follow.

> *⁴ Rejoice in the Lord always. I will say it again: Rejoice! ⁵ Let your gentleness be evident to all. The Lord is near. ⁶ Do not be anxious about anything, but in every situation, by prayer and petition, with thanksgiving, present your requests to God. ⁷ And the peace of God, which transcends all understanding, will guard your hearts and your minds in Christ Jesus.*
>
> *⁸ Finally, brothers and sisters, whatever is true, whatever is noble, whatever is right, whatever is pure, whatever is lovely, whatever is admirable—if anything is excellent or praiseworthy— think about such things. ⁹ Whatever you have learned or received or heard from me, or seen in me—put it into practice. And the God of peace will be with you.*

According to this passage, what is the remedy for anxiety? How does praying, giving thanks, and presenting your requests to God compel you to quit worrying?

When have you most recently experienced "the peace of God, which transcends all understanding" (verse 7)? How does God's supernatural peace naturally repel the enemy and keep him from getting a place at your table?

The apostle Paul urges us to focus on a number of traits that reflect God's character—including whatever is true, noble, right, pure, lovely, admirable, excellent, and praiseworthy. Yet it can be challenging to focus on such qualities if we only think of them as abstract concepts. So today, take each trait and try to think of a specific way you have witnessed or experienced God based on that quality. For example, for "true," perhaps the enemy has been trying to convince you that you're unworthy in some way. But recently, God revealed to you through the encouragement of a friend that you are loved and valued. Complete the rest with your own personal examples.

Quality	How God revealed this quality to you
True	
Noble	
Right	
Pure	
Lovely	
Admirable	
Excellent	
Praiseworthy	

DEEPER

Our Good Shepherd Has Won the Victory

"The LORD *is my shepherd, I lack nothing"* (Psalm 23:1). The enemy will try to convince you that you are living out of *lack* rather than *abundance*. He will try to convince you that you are operating from a place of defeat—that you can't move from where you are to where you want to be. Maybe you've listened to the voices of fear. Or been caught in the spiral of sin and temptation. Or convinced yourself you have no value.

The enemy has accomplished this by sitting down at your table. But you don't need to let him stay there. You do not have to entertain the enemy's voice. Through Christ, you can move to a place of victory. This happens when you learn to win the battle for your mind. Of course, the enemy knows this. So, one of his main ploys is to go after your thought life. If he can win the battle for your mind, then he can win the battle for your life.

In Numbers 13, when Moses dispatched the twelve spies to explore the land of Canaan in preparation for Hebrew conquest, ten spies returned with a fearful, faithless report. "We can't attack those people," the ten spies said, shaking in their boots. "They are stronger than we are. . . . All the people we saw there are of great size . . . We seemed like grasshoppers in our own eyes, and we looked the same to them" (verses 31, 32–33).

Hang on. How did the ten spies know what they looked like in the Canaanites' eyes? Did the spies ask their enemies, "Hey, what do you think of us? How small and puny do we look to you?" No, a seed had been planted in the spies' minds. They tended that seed and let it grow and acted on it, and as a result, they wandered in the desert for the next forty years. They never tasted the promises of God for their lives.

It didn't have to be that way, in the wilderness never tasting God's promises—not for them, and not for you and me today. Victory can be yours. Right here. Right now. Victory is about examining the seeds that have been scattered in your mind and not letting them take root. It's about pulling up and throwing away the thoughts that do not coincide with the heart of God. It's about changing the way you think.

—FROM CHAPTER 7 OF *DON'T GIVE THE ENEMY A SEAT AT YOUR TABLE*

How has the enemy tried to convince you that you are operating from a place of defeat?

How do you typically respond when you are faced with an overwhelming situation?

How can you remind yourself this week to operate out of God's strength rather than your own?

For Next Week: Before your group's next session, read chapter 8 in *Don't Give the Enemy a Seat at Your Table*.

GOD'S INVITATION ALWAYS STANDS

The enemy wants to define you by your scars. But Jesus wants to define you by His scars. The grace of Jesus Christ removes your old identity and replaces it with a brand-new identity. You are a son or daughter of God. You are a child of the King. You are written into God's will. You are a beneficiary of the lavish love of God, which has changed you from failure to family. Grace not only cancels guilt and shame—grace also redefines you. You are a beloved family member of God, and because of that you are given a seat at the table with Almighty God.

LOUIE GIGLIO
—FROM CHAPTER 8 OF *DON'T GIVE THE ENEMY A SEAT AT YOUR TABLE*

WELCOME

God's selection of Paul as the apostle to the Gentiles seems like an odd choice. Born Saul of Tarsus, he emerges on the scene not as a hero of the faith but as a persecutor of the church. We first meet him at the execution of Stephen, the first Christian martyr, watching over the proceedings and approving of everything that was done. From there, he starts dragging men and women out of their homes, putting them in prison and sentencing them to death.

Paul's encounter with the risen Christ on the road to Damascus forever changed his life. Years later, we find him penning such statements as, "There is now no condemnation for those who are in Christ Jesus" (Romans 8:1). How could Paul say this based on everything he had done? The answer is simple. Paul understood the power of *confession, repentance*, and *forgiveness*. He recognized—and believed in his heart—that Jesus had "canceled the charge" of his sins and "taken it away, nailing it to the cross" (Colossians 2:14).

Paul did not believe his past disqualified him from accepting Jesus' offer in the present. He recognized that he had been *guilty* of falling short of God's holy standard—that he was "the worst" of sinners (1 Timothy 1:15). But he did not allow that guilt to lead to *shame*. He did not allow the guilt he felt from his past to *define* who he was as a new creation in Christ.

It is important for us to recognize the depth of our sins so we can understand the mercy and grace of God. We must allow our guilt to lead to *repentance*—a 180-degree turn from the direction we were headed to the direction of our Good

Shepherd. We *can't* allow that guilt to lead us away from the dinner invitation that our King has extended to us.

SHARE

Take some time to share at least one key takeaway or insight you had from this week's personal studies. Then, to get things started, discuss one of the following questions:

- People likely considered Paul "too far gone" to be used by God. What does his story tell you about the dangers of thinking this way?

— or —

- What are some of the most notable ways that you have seen a person turn his or her life around? What led to this change in that person's life?

READ

Ask someone in the group to read aloud the following passage from James 5:13–16. Look especially for what James recommends as it relates to confession of sins.

> [13] Is anyone among you in trouble? Let them pray. Is anyone happy? Let them sing songs of praise. [14] Is anyone among you

sick? Let them call the elders of the church to pray over them and anoint them with oil in the name of the Lord. [15] And the prayer offered in faith will make the sick person well; the Lord will raise them up. If they have sinned, they will be forgiven. [16] Therefore confess your sins to each other and pray for each other so that you may be healed. The prayer of a righteous person is powerful and effective.

What are the benefits of being in community with other members of God's family?

Why does James instruct you to confess your sins to others?

Based on what you've covered in this study so far, why do you think confessing your sins to another person stops the enemy's attacks against you?

WATCH Victory Story

Play the video segment for session five. As you watch, use the following outline to record any thoughts or concepts that stand out to you.

While it's true that Jesus is alive, the grave is empty, and our future is victory through Christ, we are still in a battle. The enemy still wants to invade our thoughts and tempt us to sin. All of a sudden, we find him seated at our table.

Satan tempts us and deceives us. If we're not able to immediately defend ourselves with the Word of God, or if we're not in a community of people who can help us through that moment of temptation, we might fall. When we do fall, the most amazing thing happens. The one who tempted us in the first place becomes the one who turns around and then accuses us.

Sells us something
that isn't true
All deception
masquerades of Angel of Light

The enemy wants to convince us that we are in a unique situation. We are a special case—we are really up against it like nobody else has been—so it is okay for us to say yes to this temptation. But God wants us to know we are all on an even playing field. What has come into our lives has come into everybody else's life. He will always provide a way out.

Heaps shame + guilt
accuses us

The "way out" always starts as a big door—come to know the Almighty, get into a community of faith, get friends around you who want you to grow up in the faith. But often we pass by that door. When we do, the doors along that spiral of sin and temptation get smaller. There is still a way out, but we better act now. Go through that door!

1 Corn 10:13
No tept has seized you
what is common to man
deadly

The enemy knows that if he can put condemnation in our story, he can keep us locked into a cycle of temptation and sin. Condemnation does in our lives what it did in Adam and Eve's story. When they heard God walking in the cool of the day . . . they decided to hide from Him.

guilt
And God is faithful he will
not
But who you are he'll provide
a way out.

Conviction comes from the Holy Spirit. Condemnation comes from the enemy. Condemnation is born out of guilt, but conviction is born out of grace.

Condemnation leads us to conceal our sin. This is where Adam and Eve found themselves. But conviction leads us to confess our sin. It leads us to repentance.

Isaiah 6:5 — Isaiah seizes the Lord — I am a sinful man

Condemnation leads us to rededication—to vow over and over that we will never commit that sin again. Conviction leads us to a place of absolute and total surrender.

I can't but you can —

Condemnation leads us to a future decision that isn't going to get us where God wants us to be. But conviction is the doorway that leads us to real change in our lives.

Say hello to conviction. It's coming from the Spirit of God out of a rule of grace. Say goodbye to condemnation. It's coming from a spirit of guilt that has already been canceled in Jesus Christ.

DISCUSS

Take a few minutes within your group to discuss what you just watched and explore these concepts in Scripture.

1. God has given us the victory over the enemy through the death and resurrection of Christ. So how does the enemy still gain access to our table?

   Work.

2. Paul writes, "No temptation has overtaken you except what is common to mankind" (1 Corinthians 10:13). Why does the enemy want us to think that our situation is unique? What is the danger of thinking that our situation is "special" or that we are an "exception"?

3. What are some of the "doors" that God provides to give us a way out when we are tempted? What happens if we pass by those doors?

4. How did the enemy use condemnation in the story of Adam and Eve? How does he use condemnation today against followers of Christ?

5. Conviction comes from the Holy Spirit. What are some of the ways the Holy Spirit convicts people of sin? What typically happens as a result of that conviction?

6. Condemnation comes from the enemy. What are some of the results of giving in to feelings of condemnation? What is the remedy to breaking that cycle?

RESPOND

Briefly review the outline for the session five teaching and any notes you took. In the space below, write down your most significant takeaway from this session.

PRAY

End your session by sharing any requests that you would like the group to lift up in prayer. Thank your Good Shepherd for the invitation that He extends—in spite of your past—to dine with Him at His table. Ask that He would make you aware of the enemy's tactics so that you do not fall into condemnation. Thank the Lord that He always provides a way out when you are being tempted. Choose today to go through those doors of escape when He offers them.

Kathy - Two dr.
Ukraine
Remodel

BETWEEN-SESSIONS PERSONAL STUDY

Continue exploring the concepts you discussed during this week's group meeting by engaging in the following exercises for your personal study time. Be sure to write down any key points that stand out to you so you can share at the next meeting.

CONNECT

Check in with your group members during the upcoming week and continue the discussion you had with them at your last gathering. Grab coffee or dinner, or reach out by text and share what's going on in your heart. You can use the following questions to help guide your conversation about the battle for your mind as you overcome the enemy.

On a daily basis, how often are you aware of feeling guilt or shame for something that you have already confessed to God and know that He has forgiven? How do you handle these lingering feelings of condemnation that the enemy uses against you?

When have you recently struggled to forgive someone else for their offense against you? How have you seen the enemy use this tactic to try and get a seat at your table?

James writes, "Confess your sins to each other and pray for each other so that you may be healed" (5:16). When have you witnessed the benefits of doing this in your life?

REFLECT

Act

The enemy loves to isolate us in the guilt-and-shame quagmire of our sins—especially the ones we keep hidden. Confession enables us to break out of this isolation. It frees us from the endless cycle of sin and shame that the enemy wants to establish in our lives.

By this time, the group should hopefully be a place where you feel valued and safe to share. So, before the next session, meet with someone you trust and share one thing in your life that continues to cause you shame. Be honest, listen to the other person, and make sure to keep everything shared confidential. If this feels too great a step at the moment, then pray these words from David: "Search me, God, and know my heart; test me and know my anxious thoughts. See if there is any offensive way in me, and lead me in the way everlasting" (Psalm 139:23–24). Listen for God to lead you after you say this prayer.

Take some time after this exercise to reflect on what this meant for you.

Worship

One of the greatest prayers of confession is found in Psalm 51. Scholars believe this psalm was composed by David after he was confronted by Nathan about his adulterous affair with Bathsheba. This psalm expresses David's desire to start over with God and experience His mercy and forgiveness. Read through it slowly as you think of areas of your own life that you need to confess before the Lord. Make the words your own as you seek God's grace to restore your relationship with Him—and to overcome the taunts of the enemy in your life. Use the questions that follow to help you make this psalm your own personal prayer of repentance.

¹ Have mercy on me, O God,
    according to your unfailing love;
according to your great compassion
    blot out my transgressions.
² Wash away all my iniquity
    and cleanse me from my sin.

³ For I know my transgressions,
    and my sin is always before me.
⁴ Against you, you only, have I sinned
    and done what is evil in your sight;
so you are right in your verdict
    and justified when you judge.

⁵ Surely I was sinful at birth,
    sinful from the time my mother conceived me.
⁶ Yet you desired faithfulness even in the womb;
    you taught me wisdom in that secret place.

⁷ Cleanse me with hyssop, and I will be clean;
    wash me, and I will be whiter than snow.
⁸ Let me hear joy and gladness;
    let the bones you have crushed rejoice.
⁹ Hide your face from my sins
    and blot out all my iniquity.

¹⁰ Create in me a pure heart, O God,
    and renew a steadfast spirit within me.
¹¹ Do not cast me from your presence

> *or take your Holy Spirit from me.*
> [12] *Restore to me the joy of your salvation*
> *and grant me a willing spirit, to sustain me.*

According to the psalmist, what is the source of God's mercy?

What does the psalmist confess about himself and God's "verdict" of his sins?

What does it mean to be "restored to the joy of your salvation"?

DEEPER

Our Good Shepherd Restores Us

"He leads me beside quiet waters, he refreshes my soul" (Psalm 23:2–3). The pathway to freedom from both guilt and shame is found in the story of grace. This pathway is open to all people in the covering of grace. Grace isn't some ethereal, flimsy,

milquetoast kind of thing. Grace has grit, backbone, and muscle. Grace is the left hook that destroys the power of sin.

Shame is a powerfully destructive force. It causes us to feel we are unworthy of God's love, acceptance, or plans. It causes us to feel marred so strongly that we feel damaged beyond repair. When we feel shame, we're prone to hide. We try to hide from God behind denial or by trying to keep out of his way. Or we hide from people behind layers, walls, titles, busyness, or accomplishments. Shame imprisons each of us to the past.

It is telling that when God created the first human beings, "Adam and his wife were both naked, and they felt no shame" (Genesis 2:25). Before the fall, everything God created was described as "good," and being naked and unashamed was part of the goodness of Paradise. Yes, the garden was beautiful. Yes, there were plants and food and animals. Yes, everything was in pristine condition. But the ultimate description of goodness in Paradise was a *lack of shame*.

Then came the fall. Adam and Eve made disastrous decisions that resulted in huge consequences. Earth broke apart as a result of their choices. Both guilt and shame entered into their story—and into ours as well. One minute Adam and Eve were naked and unashamed. The next minute they were hiding from God, desperately trying to cover themselves with fig leaves.

Fortunately, God formed a rescue plan. He sheltered and clothed the two humans in garments of animal skin that He made for them. He pointed to the future and to the cross, when the serpent would harm Jesus, the Good Shepherd, by striking His heel. But Jesus would gain full victory by crushing the serpent's head. In other words, God would destroy sin and death and fully reconnect people to the purposes and person-hood of God.

Thanks to the work of Jesus on the cross, you can be free from shame. Don't let that truth pass you by. Shame does not need to be part of your story!

—FROM CHAPTER 8 OF *DON'T GIVE THE ENEMY A SEAT AT YOUR TABLE*

How would you describe God's grace at work in your life?

What were the consequences of Adam and Eve's sin that we still experience today?

How can you remind yourself this week that your past does not define you?

For Next Week: Before your group's next session, read chapters 9 and 10 in *Don't Give the Enemy a Seat at Your Table.*

IN THE PRESENCE OF OUR ENEMIES

You can win the battle for your mind. But this only happens when you surrender your life completely to Jesus. He will lead you to green pastures and quiet waters. He will guide you through dark valleys. You will not be in want, because He will restore your soul. Jesus will prepare a table for you in the presence of your enemies. But there's nothing to worry about, because your head is dripping with anointing, your cup overflows with abundance, and goodness and mercy are following you all the days of your life. The Good Shepherd is sitting at your table. Jesus has invited you to all the abundance He offers. It's a meal for the two of you.

LOUIE GIGLIO
—FROM CHAPTER 10 OF *DON'T GIVE THE ENEMY A SEAT AT YOUR TABLE*

WELCOME

The imagery of Psalm 23 is vivid and comforting. The Lord is our *shepherd*. He makes us lie down in *green pastures*. He leads us beside *quiet waters*. He guides us along the *right paths* and through the *darkest valley*. He prepares a table for us in the *presence of our enemies*.

Wait . . . what was that again? God sets the table for us in the presence of our enemies? Wouldn't it make more sense if the table was simply in *His* presence? Why do our enemies get a ringside seat? Why wouldn't God simply change the circumstances and vanquish our foes?

It's stunning when we picture it. The Good Shepherd has set a banquet table for us. Remember, this is not some rustic picnic with hot dogs and potato chips. No, we're enjoying prime rib and potatoes au gratin! We are at a feast filled with all the delicious foods that satisfy and sustain us. And we are dining with the King of kings.

Meanwhile, all around us, our enemies are prowling around watching us there at the table. The battle is still raging. We still live in a fallen world with calamities, crises, and chaos. But our Good Shepherd wants us to know that He is there with us in the midst of the pain, and the trials, and the struggles. And He wants our *enemy* to know this as well.

Paul wrote, "If God is for us, who can be against us?" (Romans 8:31). *God* is on our side. We are at the table with the wisest, kindest, most joy-filled, *and* most powerful person in the universe. Sure, the enemy is still out there, prowling like a lion. But we don't need to fear him. Instead, we can choose to stay focused on our host. As we do, we are winning the battle for our minds.

SHARE

Take some time to share at least one key takeaway or insight you had from this week's personal studies. Then, to get things started, discuss one of the following questions:

- What comes to mind when you picture God setting out a banquet table in the midst of a battlefield?

— o r —

- What does it look like to stay focused on God in the midst of the trials, battles, and struggles of your day?

READ

Ask someone in the group to read aloud the following passage from 2 Corinthians 3:12–18. Consider what Paul writes about the access that believers have to God the Father.

> ^{12} *Therefore, since we have such a hope, we are very bold.* ^{13} *We are not like Moses, who would put a veil over his face to prevent the Israelites from seeing the end of what was passing away.* ^{14} *But their minds were made dull, for to this day the same veil remains*

when the old covenant is read. It has not been removed, because only in Christ is it taken away. [15] Even to this day when Moses is read, a veil covers their hearts. [16] But whenever anyone turns to the Lord, the veil is taken away. [17] Now the Lord is the Spirit, and where the Spirit of the Lord is, there is freedom. [18] And we all, who with unveiled faces contemplate the Lord's glory, are being transformed into his image with ever-increasing glory, which comes from the Lord, who is the Spirit.

What does this passage say about the access that you have been given to God?

How does the apostle Paul say that you should approach the throne of God? How could this approach change your day-to-day relationship with Jesus?

What is the end result of spending time in God's presence?

WATCH

Play the video segment for session six. As you watch, use the following outline to record any thoughts or key points that stand out to you.

As we read David's words in Psalm 23, perhaps the most important question of all is, *why has God set a table in the presence of your enemies?* The table is not set just in God's presence—it's set in the presence of the difficulties, the trials, the challenges. So why is the table set there?

God has put the table close enough to the fray so that those in the fray can hear what is going on. Christianity is not exclusively suited for sequestered moments between us and God. It's a relationship in the *midst* of the fray so that someone who needs to know there is something called abundance can lean over and listen to what is going on between us and the King.

If we want to look different than the world, we need to put "being radiant" on our to-do list for the day. We want to have light in our eyes today—and live like there is joy in our hearts. We do this keeping our eyes locked on the King at the table instead of on the fray around us.

The table is set in the middle of our enemies so we can respond to the invitation to linger with the Savior. We don't live in a "lingering" world. But lingering in the presence of the Almighty is one of the best methods of defense against an enemy who is trying to get at our table.

So why does God set the table in the presence of our enemies? The first reason is so that **we can know that God is enough**. None of us want trials, difficulties, or moments when we feel no one has our back. But those are the moments when we recognize God is real and is with us.

The second reason for the location of the table is so **our enemies can see that God is enough**. God loves our enemies, and He wants them to have a witness. When we are looking at God, our faces reflect Him, and they begin to see God in us. We reflect God's glory.

A third reason why God put the table in the presence of our enemies **is so that we can let our cup overflow**. When we are focused on God, our cup overflows, and we have plenty of God's goodness to share with others. We find we can love our enemies, bless those who curse us, and speak well of those who are not speaking well of us.

When we are focused on God, people will notice there is something different about us. But before long, they will begin to do what we always long for people to do—stop looking at us and start trying to figure out who we are looking at. They are going to be drawn to the King.

DISCUSS

Take a few minutes within your group to discuss what you just watched and explore these concepts in Scripture.

1. When have you experienced God's presence unexpectedly in the midst of a difficult time? How did your awareness of His presence affect your response to the situation?

2. What is the difference between knowing *about* God and knowing Him on a *personal* basis? What are some ways that you seek to better know God personally?

3. Why is "lingering" so counterintuitive in today's world? What would it look like for you to "linger" in God's presence? What obstacles would you have to overcome to do this?

4. How would you summarize the reason why God puts the table in the presence of your *enemies*? How does the "location" of this table impact your life and the lives of others?

5. David wrote, "I sought the LORD, and he answered me; he delivered me from all my fears" (Psalm 34:4). What is the impact on others when they witness God showing up in this manner and delivering you from all your fears?

6. David continued, "Those who look to him are radiant; their faces are never covered with shame" (Psalm 34:5). How are you staying focused on the King at your table regardless of what is happening around you in your world?

RESPOND

Briefly review the outline for the session six teaching and any notes you took. In the space below, write down your most significant takeaway from this session.

PRAY

End your session by sharing any requests that you would like the group to lift up in prayer. Close with a time of thanksgiving to God, just lingering in His presence for a few minutes. Praise Him for the gift of Jesus, your Good Shepherd, and for the victory you have been given through His death and resurrection. Ask the Lord to continue to show you ways the enemy tries to get a seat at your table so that you can always be prepared to counter his strategies.

FINAL

PERSONAL STUDY

Continue exploring the concepts you discussed during this week's group meeting by engaging in the following exercises for your personal study time. Be sure to write down any key points that stand out to you.

CONNECT

Check in with your group one last time to discuss what you learned and celebrate what God has done during the past six weeks. Grab coffee or dinner, or reach out by text and share what's going on in your heart. Try to make sure that everyone in your group hears from someone else. Reflect on the questions below on what you've learned about winning the battle for your mind during this study.

How do you feel about turning the enemy away now that you have completed this study?

What have you learned about the enemy's tactics in trying to get a seat at your table?

What strategies have you learned to keep him from getting a place there?

REFLECT

Act

Look back through your notes, questions, and reflections that you have written down, both from your group meetings and from your personal study in between sessions. Then answer the following questions as you evaluate your experience during this study.

How has your relationship with God changed during the course of this study? Where do you see evidence of this change as you review your notes, answers, and written reflections?

How has the battle for control of your thoughts changed since you started this study? What have you learned about God and how you relate to Him?

What passage or verses from God's Word has empowered you the most as you battle the enemy? Why do you think that truth from the Bible means so much to you?

Worship

God speaks to us through passages of Scripture in different ways and at different times. Now that you've completed this study, spend a few minutes reflecting on Psalm 23 one more time. Read through each sentence of the psalm below, and then answer the corresponding question. Go slowly as you do this and just take some time to linger in God's presence.

"The Lord is my shepherd, I lack nothing" (Psalm 23:1). How does knowing that God will provide for your needs give you comfort and security?

"He makes me lie down in green pastures, he leads me beside quiet waters, he refreshes my soul" (Psalm 23:2–3). When has the Lord made you "lie down" in order to refresh your soul? How would you describe this time of spiritual refreshment?

"He guides me along the right paths for his name's sake" (Psalm 23:3). How have you seen God guide you along the right paths in this life?

"Even though I walk through the darkest valley, I will fear no evil, for you are with me; your rod and your staff, they comfort me" (Psalm 23:4). How has the Good Shepherd protected you and dispelled your fears when you have walked through life's dark valleys?

"You prepare a table before me in the presence of my enemies" (Psalm 23:5). What image comes to mind when you read this verse? How has your understanding of this verse changed since you have gone through this study?

"You anoint my head with oil; my cup overflows" (Psalm 23:5). What are some of the ways that God has made your cup "overflow"? How are you sharing this overflow with others?

"Surely your goodness and love will follow me all the days of my life, and I will dwell in the house of the LORD forever" (Psalm 23:6). How have you seen God's goodness "following you" in your life? What hope do you gain by knowing you will dwell in God's house forever?

DEEPER

Our Good Shepherd Gives Us Abundant Life

"Surely your goodness and love will follow me all the days of my life" (Psalm 23:6). When Jesus lives in you, your slate is clean. You are set free from condemnation. You are given a new life and placed into a new family. You have a relationship with God through Jesus. As a result, you experience the abundant life that Jesus promised: "The thief comes only to steal and kill and destroy; I have come that they may have life, and have it to the full" (John 10:10).

Christ's work on the cross got you out of death, so now your life can be lived fully surrendered to Him. You are alive in the Spirit, alive by the Spirit, alive for Christ, alive in Christ, to live the life of Christ so that He might be glorified. This is not a negotiation. This is a call to surrender completely to Jesus. You are to be completely open and available to Him. He has given you a new identity. Your call is to make Him known in the world.

I don't know about you, but I want to daily set my mind and heart on Christ. I want to constantly fill my mind with Scripture. I want God to move in a supernatural way. I don't want to get to the end of my days and look back to see a cookie-cutter existence that looks like what society says a normal life should be. I don't want the easiest path. I want to know God intimately. I want my life to be abundant and defy human explanation.

I'm thinking this is the life you want too. This kind of life can be yours. One that's dependent fully on the power of the Holy Spirit. And it's activated by you stepping forward in faith. Too often we want to see miracles first before we take a step. But the fullness of the life that Jesus provides becomes evident when we move, act on His leading, and open our mouths and speak. The steps we take in faith activate the power of the Spirit.

That's your call today. Do not give the enemy a seat at your table. You *can* win the battle for your mind. The Good Shepherd *is* sitting at your table. Jesus has invited you to all the abundance He offers. It's a meal for just the two of you. He Himself is the feast.

—FROM CHAPTER 10 OF *DON'T GIVE THE ENEMY A SEAT AT YOUR TABLE*

What evidence can others see that Jesus lives inside of you?

What do you want to be able to say about your life when you get to the end of your days?

What step do you sense God is asking you to take today to experience the full life He offers?

LEADER'S GUIDE

Thank you for your willingness to lead your group through this study. What you have chosen to do is valuable and will make a great difference in the lives of others. The rewards of being a leader are different from those of participating, and we hope that as you lead you will find your own walk with Jesus deepened by the experience.

Don't Give the Enemy a Seat at Your Table is a six-session Bible study based on Psalm 23 that is built around video content and small-group interaction. As the group leader, imagine yourself as the host of a dinner party. Your job is to take care of your guests by managing the behind-the-scenes details so that as your guests arrive, they can focus on one another and on the interaction around the topic for that week.

As the group leader, your role is not to answer all the questions or reteach the content—the video, book, and study guide will do most of that work. Your job is to guide the experience and cultivate your small group into a connected and engaged community. This will make it a place for members to process, question, and reflect—not receive more instruction.

There are several elements in this leader's guide that will help you as you structure your study and reflection time, so be sure to follow along and take advantage of each one.

BEFORE YOU BEGIN

Before your first meeting, make sure the group members have a copy of this study guide so they can follow along and have their answers written out ahead of time. Alternately, you can hand out the study guides at your first meeting and give the group members some time to look over the material and ask any preliminary questions. During your first meeting, be sure to send a sheet of paper around the room and have the members write down their name, phone number, and email address so you can keep in touch with them during the week.

Generally, the ideal size for a group is eight to ten people, which will ensure that everyone has enough time to participate in discussions. If you have more people, you might want to break up the main group into smaller subgroups. Encourage those who show up at the first meeting to commit to attending the duration of the study, as this will help the group members get to know one another, create stability for the group, and help you as the leader know how to best prepare each week.

Each of the sessions begins with an opening reflection. The questions that follow in the "Share" section serve as an icebreaker to get the group members thinking about the general topic at hand. Some people may want to tell a long story in response to one of these questions, but the goal is to keep the answers brief. Ideally, you want everyone in the group to get a chance to answer, so try to keep the responses to a minute or less. If you have talkative group members, say up front that everyone needs to limit the answer to one minute.

Give the group members a chance to answer, but tell them to feel free to pass if they wish. With the rest of the study, it's generally not a good idea to have everyone answer every question—a free-flowing discussion is more desirable. But with the opening icebreaker-type questions, you can go around the circle. Encourage shy people to share, but don't force them.

At your first meeting, let the group members know each session contains a personal study section that they can use to reflect more on the content during the week. While this is an optional exercise, it will help the members cement the concepts presented during the group study time and encourage them to spend time each day in God's Word. Invite them to bring any questions and insights they uncovered while reading to your next meeting, especially if they had a breakthrough moment or didn't understand something.

WEEKLY PREPARATION

As the leader, there are a few things you should do to prepare for each meeting:

- *Read through the session.* This will help you to become more familiar with the content and know how to structure the discussion times.
- *Decide which questions you definitely want to discuss.* Based on the amount and length of group discussion, you may not be able to get through all the questions, so choose four to five that you definitely want to cover.
- *Be familiar with the questions you want to discuss.* When the group meets you'll be watching the clock, so you want to make sure you are familiar with the questions you have selected. In this way, you'll ensure you have the material more deeply in your mind than your group members.
- *Pray for your group.* Pray for your group members throughout the week and ask God to lead them as they study His Word.

In many cases, there will be no one "right" answer to the question. Answers will vary, especially when the group members are being asked to share their personal experiences.

STRUCTURING THE DISCUSSION TIME

You will need to determine with your group how long you want to meet each week so you can plan your time accordingly. Generally, most groups like to meet for either ninety minutes or two hours, so you could use one of the following schedules:

Section	90 Minutes	120 Minutes
Welcome (members arrive and get settled)	10 minutes	15 minutes
Share (discuss one or more of the opening questions for the session)	15 minutes	20 minutes
Watch (watch the teaching material together and take notes)	25 minutes	25 minutes
Discuss (discuss the Bible study questions you selected ahead of time)	30 minutes	45 minutes
Respond / Pray (reflect on the message, pray together as a group, and dismiss)	10 minutes	15 minutes

As the group leader, it is up to you to keep track of the time and keep things on schedule. You might want to set a timer for each segment so both you and the group members know when your time is up. (There are some good phone apps for timers that play a gentle chime or other pleasant sound instead of a disruptive noise.)

Don't be concerned if the group members are quiet or slow to share. People are often quiet when they are pulling together their ideas, and this might be a new experience for them. Just ask a question and let it hang in the air until someone shares. You can then say, "Thank you. What about others? What came to you when you watched that portion of the teaching?"

GROUP DYNAMICS

Leading a group through *Don't Give the Enemy a Seat at Your Table* will prove to be highly rewarding both to you and your group members. But you still may encounter challenges along the way! Discussions can get off track. Group members may not be sensitive to the needs and ideas of others. Some might worry they will be expected to talk about matters that make them feel awkward. Others may express comments that result in disagreements. To help ease this strain on you and the group, consider the following ground rules:

- When someone raises a question or comment that is off the main topic, suggest you deal with it another time, or, if you feel led to go in that direction, let the group know you will be spending some time discussing it.
- If someone asks a question that you don't know how to answer, admit it and move on. At your discretion, feel free to invite group members to comment on questions that call for personal experience.
- If you find one or two people are dominating the discussion time, direct a few questions to others in the group. Outside the main group time, ask the more dominating members to help you draw out the quieter ones. Work to make them a part of the solution instead of the problem.
- When a disagreement occurs, encourage the group members to process the matter in love. Encourage those on opposite sides to restate what they heard the other side say about the matter, and then invite each side to

evaluate if that perception is accurate. Lead the group in examining other Scriptures related to the topic and look for common ground.

When any of these issues arise, encourage your group members to follow these words from the Bible: "Love one another" (John 13:34), "If it is possible, as far as it depends on you, live at peace with everyone" (Romans 12:18), "Whatever is true . . . noble . . . right . . . if anything is excellent or praiseworthy— think about such things" (Philippians 4:8), and "Be quick to listen, slow to speak and slow to become angry" (James 1:19). This will make your group time more rewarding and beneficial for everyone who attends.

Thank you again for your willingness to lead your group. May God reward your efforts and dedication, equip you to guide your group in the weeks ahead, and make your time together in *Don't Give the Enemy a Seat at Your Table* fruitful for His kingdom.

COMPANION BOOK TO ENRICH YOUR STUDY EXPERIENCE

DON'T GIVE THE ENEMY A SEAT AT YOUR TABLE

IT'S TIME TO WIN THE BATTLE OF YOUR MIND...

LOUIE GIGLIO

ISBN 9780785247227

Available wherever books are sold